DATE DUE

JA 20'06			

Heartbreak and Roses

revised edition

Real Life Stories of Troubled Love

janet bode

and

stan mack

Franklin Watts

New York / London / Sydney / Hong Kong

Danbury, Connecticut

To Carole Mayedo

Visit Franklin Watts on the Internet at
http://publishing.grolier.com

Book production by Editorial Directions, Inc.
Jacket and book design by Marie O'Neill.
Cover and interior photos of man ©Corbis, and rose ©PhotoDisc:Emanuele Taroni

Library of Congress Cataloging-in-Publication Data
Bode, Janet.
    Heartbreak and roses : real life stories of troubled love / by Janet Bode and Stan Mack.
    —Rev. ed.
      p. cm.
    Includes bibliographical references and index.
    Summary : Teens from around the United States reflect on love, sexual behavior, and relationships with their parents and friends.
    ISBN 0-531-11776-6 (lib. bdg.)   0-531-16464-0 (pbk.)
    1. Teenagers—United States—Sexual behavior—Juvenile literature. 2. Interpersonal relations in adolescence—United States—Juvenile literature. 3. Parents and teenager—United States—Juvenile literature. [1. Youth—Sexual behavior. 2. Interpersonal relations. 3. Parent and child. 4. Love.] I. Mack, Stanley, ill. II. Title.
    HQ27.B616 2000
    306.7'0835—dc21
                                         99-38550
                                         CIP

Part One

tEn
MinutEs
ON
L●VE

The idea for *Heartbreak and Roses* started with you. When I meet with teenagers to talk about books, I leave time to learn what's on your mind. Some of you want to do this as a conversation. Others want more privacy. You tell me "yes" when I ask, "Are you willing to write about your life for ten minutes?"

I always repeat, "It's your choice to write or not. And you don't have to sign any name or you can make one up." Even though we've spent the last hour together, I'm a stranger asking personal questions. Still, time after time almost everyone in the room picks up paper and a pen. When I get home and read what you have to say, I see a recurring theme: love troubles.

Here you'll find a collection of these troubled love mini-autobiographies from eighth graders to high school seniors around the country. Think of these typical responses as quick comments a good friend tells you. Hearing them may start you thinking about your own love connections. And maybe they'll start you seeing them more clearly.

—*Janet Bode*

My life is going pretty well, except I'm lonely.

I walk through the halls and see so many couples.

All I need is to find a girl I want to be with. Doesn't sound so hard, huh? Still, it seems impossible. I guess I should just wait my turn. But the question is, how long?

tEn MinutEs ON LOVE

For one year and two months I've been going out with Sean. Lately, I'm opening my eyes and seeing a jerk. He's guided by his ego and pride. He doesn't appreciate me, but he expects me to stick around. I'm scared, though. He knows extremely personal things about me. If I break up with him, afterward he'll probably spread stories. I'm so confused.

Typical Situation

This cartoon strip is a student-created project for a class assignment. See Part Three for more information.

Last week my boyfriend was going to love me forever. "Let's get married," he was always saying. Now he just left me for another girl. He hasn't even contacted me to break-up officially. It's like I no longer exist in his world. And I have no idea what made him change in a few days.

Maybe it's because he has self-destructive behavior and does drugs. I couldn't make him stop even when he knew it bothered me. He solemnly swore to quit or not do them around me. Then he slipped and did it anyway. Writing about this makes me feel better. I hope the more I review these events on paper and with my friends the more I'll be able to figure them out. Right now, though, I admit it, all I feel like doing is crying.

•Next period she and I had the same study hall, coinncidentially, we were across from each other....

A friend framed us together...

Cat

I've been seeing a girl for a month and then she hears rumors from a jealous friend. So my girlfriend goes all mad and for three days doesn't even tell me why. This morning she accuses me

I'm a sophomore and in September I was new to the "big" high school. I made friends quite fast and was on the school kick-line team. One afternoon I was waiting with a friend for dance practice to start. I went down the hall to get a drink and there was this guy and a group of his friends that I'd seen before but never spoken to. He had deep-set eyes that really scared me.

As I walked passed him, he started to follow me. He came up behind and put his arm around me. "Whose property are you?" he said. I looked at him strongly—like "get away," but he persisted. He started kissing my neck and said, "Come on, you know you want me."

His friends were forming a tight circle around

of having sex with another girl and doesn't even want my side of the story. Now she hates me. All her friends hate me, and I didn't do anything!

us. There was no one to help me. Finally I started to scream, "Leave me alone!" He let me go, but the memories stay. I get a flash about it. I can't sleep some nights. Trying to deal with this is terrible.

CHAKIRA

I went out with this guy, Bobby, in October. Then we broke up, but I still love him. I think about him so much, it's getting me sick. My family could care less. They just say, "Chakira, are you ready to come out of your room now?"

I was going to a therapist until my stepmother refused to take me anymore. She wants me to move back with my mom. I can't trust my friends, especially about Bobby. They're backstabbers. I have no one to talk to.

TOMMY

The best thing happening in my life is my girlfriend just had our son. It was an unplanned mistake. She is only sixteen and I am eighteen. To celebrate being a father I got my first deer this hunting season. The worst thing is that my truck broke down today. I have no money to fix it and now I have no way to get around.

CELESTE

I have a messed-up life with divorced parents and a hateful stepdad. At the same moment I have Alan, a very nice guy, on my mind. We talk over the Internet. We don't know what each other looks like which is just fine with me. He tells me he loves me for who I am, not what's on the outside. Alan is someone I can talk to. And I have always wanted a boyfriend like that.

"That weekend we went to see a movie The typical date idea.

I didn't have a better idea so we went.

We got to the theatre and I was nervous as any thing...

Sitting there, I wasn't sure of the expectations, so I sat nervously

I felt stupid and wanted to leave after a while.

Later she told me that she didn't want to go out again. I was very...

Sad.

For the next few weeks were we pretty awkward. We got back together and ended up on and off for about 3 months.

Things were never the same.

The End

Part Two

LOVE TROUBLES

thE dETAiLS

After reading those paragraphs about love, after thinking about the cartoon, I started to interview individual teenagers willing to discuss their lives in detail. Some talked of love gone wrong—violent love, obsessive love, tormented love leading to suicide attempts. Others had real-life stories of bittersweet love—

battles for love when everyone and everything seemed to be against them.

As in life, and especially life in the teen years, the course of love in those tales was often turbulent. After the first edition came out, you wrote to tell me that some of the stories upset you. Two in particular caused the most controversy, "Love on the Run" where Kirsten falls madly in love with a skinhead and "Undercover Love" where Seth discovers he loves his best friend, Zach.

YOUR JUDGMENTS

You thought I should step in and make a value judgment—about skinheads and about gay and lesbian love. But the original *Heartbreak and Roses* and this new edition are books for and about you. What's important is how you react to the stories, how they affect your emotions, your judgments, and your sense of self. Other stories, you said, comfort you. They help you see your own love problems more clearly. They also help you realize that your love troubles are minor compared to those of your peers.

I purposely looked for students with different backgrounds. Whether you supported or were outraged by the lives they lead, these adolescents remain part of our human family. And, therefore, I included them on these pages. My main goal, though, was to provide you with a collection of stories so dramatic that it opened the door to your imagination and let you read them the way you'd read the best fiction. At times, maybe you even have to remind yourself, those were the words of real teenagers.

To protect the identities of the people I interviewed, I changed their names and altered some details, but not enough to take away from the fact that the heart of their experiences were completely true.

Heartbreak and Roses

Bonnie

For nine months after Michael and I **BROKE UP,** I didn't want to talk to a guy on the phone. **I didn't want** a guy to put his arm around me. I didn't want **to go near another guy.**

My friends were, like, "You know, Bonnie, all guys aren't the same."

But Michael changed my life.

He made me scared of guys, scared that someday every guy will change, too. The way Michael did.

Now I've been going out with Vince for about two months. He's nice to me. Still, I think, "What if we get into a fight or something? Is he going to hit me?"

I can't help it. I get nervous. Every time I'm with Vince, I get flashbacks of Michael. Michael would pressure me into sex.

The one time Vince and I tried to have sex, it was totally different from Michael. Still, I "saw" Michael hitting me. I said, "I have to stop."

"That's okay," Vince said, before asking, "What happened with Michael?"

I told him. I moved here from Michigan to live with my mom. I didn't have many friends, but this one girl, Jacklynn, went to a church that was having a teen weekend. A whole bunch of kids would get together and spend the night at the church.

That's where I met Michael. The first thing I notice was he was cute. Honestly I can say I started staring at him. He had a girlfriend, but he kept looking back at me.

When the weekend was over, I went to Jacklynn's to search through her yearbook. There he was. We were both going into eighth grade.

You know how guys like girls who are new in school. There were guys who liked me. But there was something about Michael that I liked more. We started going out and stuff.

ALONE

Six months go by, and everything is fine. We are together every day. We don't fight. The most he does is get mad if another guy looks at me.

One day he says, "Bonnie, to tell you the truth, my first intention was to use you."

"What's that supposed to mean?" I ask him.

"All my friends wanted to go out with you. I wanted to be, 'Well, I have her.' But I've ended up falling in love with you."

Then we have sex. We are each other's first. He starts getting more possessive.

It's so gradual, piece by piece; I don't really notice. When I do, I tell myself, "Michael's doing it because he loves me so much." I tell him, "Sometimes I want to hang out with my girlfriends."

He's, like, "They're losers. Anyway, they talk behind your back."

"I want a social life. I want to have my own friends."

"I want you all to myself," he says. "I sleep with your picture."

Meanwhile, he's out cheating behind my back. My mom and I are shopping, and I see him walking down the street holding hands with some girl. I start crying. He's always saying, "I could get other girls easy if I wasn't going out with you."

Instead of yelling at him, I yell at the girls.

When Michael and I have sex, he never uses anything. He says, "I don't feel like it and you can't make me anyway." The time I think I might be pregnant, he says, "Just tell your mom you got raped." When I yell at him for that, he apologizes.

I'll tell you what, I prayed that night, "God, please don't let me be pregnant." I did the whole rosary. The next morning, I got my period. I said, "Thank you, God."

CONTROL

Michael told me what to wear and what not to wear. If I wore something he didn't approve of, he would make me put on his sweatshirt. My mom bought me an outfit for my birthday. The shirt was a little short. Michael said, "Wear a tank top under it."

I told him, "No."

I wore it to school the way I liked it, and when he saw me, he started screaming, "You slut," in front of everybody.

"Get out of this relationship," I told myself. I don't know why, but I just couldn't do it. After each fight, Michael would bring me a dozen roses.

I start marking in my diary the days that Michael hits me. It gets to be once or twice a week. I leave my diary out, figuring, you know how moms are. She'll probably read it.

If she does, we never really talk about it.

Instead I make up answers. When she asks about my latest bruise, I tell her, "Oh, I fell off the couch." I tell myself the same old thing: "Bonnie, this relationship is no good for you." For that whole year, I can't get out. I guess I like him too much.

He shows up at my house with some of his friends. My mom says I can't have guys in if she's not here. Michael knows that. When I won't let him in, he starts hitting the door until it breaks.

He charges in, throwing things, saying, "I'm going to kill you." He picks up the phone and begins to tell all his friends to come by. When I try to stop him, he hits me over the head with the receiver.

I black out and come to.

"Get out!" I scream. I call his dad and say, "Can you come

over and pick up your son?" By the time his dad gets here, everyone's gone. He doesn't believe me about what happened.

Later that day, Michael is on the phone to me. He says, "I'm sorry. I don't know what came over me." The next day, he stops by when my mom is at work. He hands me a dozen roses, and he leaves.

Everything is fine again, I think.

THREATS

For the last six months of our relationship, we'd break up at least once a week. Anything you could think of, he'd fight about. Like, my mom didn't want me talking on the phone after nine o'clock.

He'd call whenever he felt like it. If the line was busy, he'd do an emergency breakthrough. Then he'd scream, "You better be around to talk to me when I want you!"

One night my mom finally took the phone off the hook. We didn't know that my grandma was trying to get hold of us to say that my mother's brother had died.

Of course, I was upset. I called Michael the next day, saying my uncle died and they couldn't get through, 'cause the line was busy.

"Who cares," he said.

That was it! I was devastated. I told him, "We're over."

He said, "You break up with me, I'm going to kill myself." I didn't believe him.

The next day, he called up and said, "I just slit my wrist." I ran all the way to his house. Hysterical. I opened his door. He was lying there on the floor with a towel around his hand.

I said, "Oh, no, please say you didn't." I pulled the towel off his hand and—nothing.

He said, "Now that I have you, I'm not going to let you go." There was nobody else at his house.

I said, "Please, just let me go on with my life."

"No, Bonnie," he said, "you are my life."

I was scared. I tried to get past him and out the front door. He grabbed me. He slapped me across the face. He got me in a choke hold. I started crying. Then he started crying.

He said, "Bonnie, I love you. I didn't mean to do that. I'm so sorry."

"I can't take it," I said. "I want out." His mood changed in a heartbeat.

"You want out of here?" he said. "Fine. Fine." He pushed me off the top step of the front porch.

I started walking home, and then I realized, "Well, he said he loved me. Maybe he just needs me."

I thought maybe I wasn't good enough for him.

I imagined following him everywhere, begging him, "Please, forgive me. I'll do everything you want."

Why did I want him back?

Why did I feel it was my fault?

Why did I feel I was nothing without him?

I don't know. What I know is he was my first love. Maybe I drove him to the violence.

He called me and called me. When I finally gave in and called him back, he screamed, "What do you want!" at the top of his lungs.

DEPROGRAMMING MYSELF

That day it just clicks into me: Michael doesn't think about anybody but himself. There are plenty of guys out there. I shouldn't be abused. I'm only fourteen years old.

I tell him over the phone, "We have to break up."

"No other guy will love you as much as I do," he says.

The more I think about him and our relationship, the more upset I am. I look at my diary again and again. I'm used to having him around. I think about getting back together.

I stay in my room the whole weekend. I make myself remember each time he's hit me. Each time he's screamed at me. Each time he's pressured me to have sex. Each time I've heard he's cheated on me. Each time I can't do something because of him.

I have to, like, deprogram myself to fall out of love with him.

I start trying to make friends. When I begin to tell Jacklynn some of the details, she cries with me.

I try to put Michael out of my mind as much as I can.

I keep myself occupied.

I talk to my mom.

When I want to call him, I call someone else.

I write in my diary about my feelings.

I go run around the track at school until I can hardly walk.

I make dinner.

I listen to other people's problems.

I pray to God to help me be strong.

PICTURE-PERFECT

It's been nearly a year since Michael. Sometimes I feel he's on my shoulder when Vince and I are together.

He's saying, "Bonnie, how could you do this? You know I still love you."

I say to myself, "Don't think about him."

Vince thinks it's no big deal that I hang out with my friends. He likes them, too. We all spend time together.

I have my first job. My mom leaves me a note in the morning. She says, "Dear Bonnie, I want to see my little girl on her first day of work. Please have Vince take your picture."

I tell him, "Don't bother. I look stupid in this outfit I have to wear."

Vince says, "You look cute! You always do."

"Go ahead and take my picture," I say, and smile in a way that shows I'm going to be okay.

The Class Flirt
Meets His Match

Louis

My last year at
middle school, I was
voted **class flirt.**
I was the sweet talker,
the **wanderer.**
I'd never settle down.
One night a
week, the guys and I
had a condom run.
We'd buy different
kinds and trade them.

I like hanging out with the guys. I really like girls, too. For some reason I can talk to them. I can cry, too. I have no idea why. Girls love it though. It's the way guys should be.

One night that summer before tenth grade, I was at the carnival with a bunch of buddies. When I saw this girl, I said to my friend Tom, "She is so hot."

"She'll never give you the time of day," he said.

"We'll see about that," I told him.

She was playing this game where you throw a softball at a target. I'd won it, like, twelve times. She was on her third ball. I knew she was going to miss.

I ran up to her and said, "You're doing it all wrong! Stand over here. It's my lucky spot."

"Why don't you do it?" she said.

"No, you can."

She threw the ball, and she won!

I said, "Well, since you won, I have to give you my phone number." She smiled and took it. Her name, she told me, was Maura.

The next day, I was at her front door. She had a boyfriend but was in the process of breaking up with him. I asked her out. It never occurred to me she might be a world-class flirt herself.

KISSING MAURA

When I met Maura, she's thirteen. I'm sixteen. She tells me she's fourteen, going to be fifteen. Much later I ask her, "How come you lied to me?"

She goes, "Would you really have stood there and talked to a thirteen-year-old?"

Back in the very beginning, she says, "What would be the perfect girl for you?"

"Cause I'm a player, no girl has ever trusted me. For a girl to look me in the eye and tell me that she actually trusts me—wow."

"Louis," she says, "I trust you."

From then on, for me everything revolves around Maura. I'm spending all my money and my time on her until my mom says, "I thought you were saving for a car?"

I say, "Yeah, I'll save." I put a couple of bucks away, and then I end up blowing it. I buy Maura presents. I take her out to dinner, to the movies, to the beach.

Two o'clock in the morning when I leave work, I detour to her house. I knock on her window to tell her sweet dreams and kiss her goodnight.

Let me tell you, I can spend hours just kissing Maura. I let my tongue caress every part of her lips. I kiss the top one, the bottom one, then trace along them to the corners where they meet. I'm always gentle with her. With my touch I tell her how I feel.

OBSESSION

There are dances at her middle school. I say, "Go ahead."

She says, "Only if you're out in the parking lot waiting for me." So I'm out there, acting like a jerk, waiting for her. First the security guards just kick me off the property. Then I get trespassing cards. Next I'm almost arrested.

My buddy Tom says, "Come on, Louis, let's go shoot some baskets." I think about it for two seconds until Maura comes by. I leave my friends.

They try not to get mad at me, but I start hearing from them, "You're ditching us, and for a younger girl."

Maura and I get into trouble because we never do anything

with our families anymore, either. My mom's worried. She thinks we're spending too much time together. I tell her, "You don't know what you're talking about."

Her mom says, "Don't you hang out with anyone else?"

My mom starts in on the pregnancy lectures. "Maura's a little girl. Don't forget that. If she gets pregnant, you're in deep trouble."

I say, "Don't worry!"

"I'm your mother," she says. "I'm supposed to worry."

Her dad starts being pretty rude. He's, like, "Louis is three years older, and he's too perfect." I guess he thinks the nicer a guy is, the further he'll get with his daughter.

EXPLORATION

If they only knew. When it came to sex and stuff, Maura was pushy. She was the virgin. I wasn't. She started asking me when we would do it.

I said, "You don't have to do that." I thought that she might have felt obligated to do something because she was younger with an older guy.

She kept bringing it up. "Well, what does it feel like?" she'd ask.

"Come on," I said. "I'm not a girl. I can't tell you that much."

She was hanging out with older girls, the wild dressers. I didn't know what they talked about behind closed doors, but they filled her head up with the message: Do it!

Don't get me wrong. I thought sex was great. But there were times when not having sex could be great in its own way.

Like, we were in my room, lying on my bed. I was on the bottom, Maura on top. We were kissing and kissing, and after a while my hands started exploring. I touched her hair, her neck, her shoulders, her back.

I ran my fingers over her clothes, over her skin. I brushed my cheeks and my lips along her arms and those thighs of hers. She had these tiny, golden hairs on her legs that kind of teased me. The ache I felt for her was intense.

See, before all this my mom and I had been close. She knows what's going on. She's the one who talks to me about sex and all that. Not so much my dad. He only jokes about it. Instead of a condom, he says, "Don't forget your umbrella."

My mom says, "Guys can be pressured, too. Listen to your best judgment, not your hormones. When you're ready, you'll know. Maura may think she's ready, but afterward she could regret it."

POSSESSION

One night after we'd been going out for almost three months, Maura goes, "I really want to do it."

I say, "You'll chicken out."

Then she says, "Do you have condoms?"

I tell her, "I'm not stupid. I'm always prepared."

The next day when she comes over, she finds my condoms. I have this rule. If a girl and I are about to have sex, I will never open up a condom.

I think for a guy to do that makes it look like he wants it too much. Then if he opens it and the girl says no, the guy gets mad at her.

We're fooling around and Maura opens a condom. I'm thinking, "Ohmigosh."

She says, "You know this is my first time."

From then on, it gets out of hand. We have sex a couple of

times a week. I'm scared she'll get pregnant. She doesn't seem to care.

One day she says, "Should we stop using condoms?"

I'm thinking, "Everybody's always saying it feels better without it." And I'm sure it does. When I think of my future, I see a wife and two kids. Maura, of course, is the wife.

I get a wonderful feeling at the thought of being the father of her children. We'd make new lives—together—and I'd love them as much as I love their mother.

That's the future. This is now.

"No," I tell her. "For now we can't make love without a condom."

She's actually glad I wear it. It proves how much I care about her. I'd never do anything to hurt her. I feel like there's nothing else in my life, just her.

RUMORS

At a New Year's Eve party, Maura noticed this guy Richard. He was flirting with her. Was she coming on to him?

Richard! The kid across the street. I grew up with him. I taught him everything. He's a smooth talker. He's younger than me and in her school. He would see her more than me during the school day. I felt like a dummy.

It's hard to trust your friends when it comes to a girl. There are more guys who'll stab their friends over that. Even if the guy says no, if the girl is good-looking, really sweet and cherry, it's what every guy wants.

Four and a half months into our relationship, Maura's feelings were turning towards him. I started worrying, "I'm going to lose you."

She was, like, "No, you won't."

The worrying turned into arguing. I said, "You're going to end up with Richard."

"No I'm not!"

"Yes, you are!"

Everything was going downhill.

Maura said, "Why don't you go look at the girls in high school?"

"But I love you," I told her.

Every day I heard a new rumor. Richard screwed her over. She was with this guy Adam. I didn't believe what anybody told me. I had too much trust in her. She wouldn't break up with me.

It was tearing me apart.

I felt that we had something good going and we were throwing it away for nothing. I call her up and say, "I know you want to break up with me. Why don't you do it?"

She says, "I still love you."

I think, If she loves me, can she care about Richard? I say, "Well, who is it? Me? Richard? Adam? Some other guy altogether?"

"You," she says.

I go, "Why are you lying to me?" We start to really argue then, and finally I say, "It's over!" She starts crying.

After it's officially over, we stay on the phone for another four hours. I even warn her how certain guys are when it comes to sex. "Some are out for one thing. They figure if you've lost your virginity, they can go do it with you."

By the end of the conversation, it's like nothing ever happened. We're back together.

Then two days later, she's going out with some other kid! Her friends are telling me, "Louis, she's a flirt."

One of them says, "She told me she's using the guy to get over you."

I was going crazy.

IN LOVE

Maura called. She felt it'd be better if she gave me back my chain and stuff. I went over to her house.

Along with the chain, she handed me a poem she started the night before. It was called "Trapped in Love." She said she was stuck on the last sentence.

I tell her, "Don't finish it. I will."

I wanted to write how I felt right then. How it didn't matter what we talked about. How I just wanted to follow her with my eyes. How I wanted time to stop to keep the memory fresh.

Was I loving her so much that it made her feel trapped?

By then we were both crying. She says, "I still love you."

When she kisses me, I say, "You can't do that. I'm trying to get over you."

She says, "Why did we mess up? You're the only guy who never hurt me."

The phone rang. She went to answer it. From the other room I could hear her talking. She said some guy's name. She laughed at something he must have said.

I recognized her voice. It was the voice I thought she saved only for me. She was sweet-talking this guy. She was flirting with him.

I went home in shock.

REENTRY

I know now that a girlfriend or boyfriend is just that. They are not life. You don't have to be with them twenty-four hours a day, seven days a week. You have other friends, too.

Even when you love the person, she's still a friend, which means she can hang out with your other friends. They're bound to have something in common. If they don't, you should wonder, is there a problem?

In the months I was with Maura, I'll never know how much I missed out on. My friends would say, "Yeah, man, we went to this party. You missed the fun."

You should listen to your family. Ignore them, they're going to ignore you. And you need them.

Once Tom and my other friends found out we'd broken up for good, they did call. They didn't remind me too often that I was a jerk to forget about everybody for Maura. And then look how she treated me, they'd add.

SELF-PROTECTION

Maura's been calling. In her messages she says, "You're never home. All I get is your answering machine. How come you don't call me?"

One day she catches me in. I go, "Yeah, I get your messages."

"Louis," she says, "I can't live without you. And I know you can't live without me."

I get mad that she says that. I'm, like, "Wait a second. I'm seeing a girl right now. I'm living without you, aren't I?"

Still, she knows she's right. I only say that to protect myself.

May 2, 1997. The *New York Times*, AP.

Sex Activity by Youths Is on Decline

The proportion of American teen-agers who have had sexual intercourse at least once has dropped for the first time in more than 20 years, the government reported today.

The finding came from two surveys. One of them found that 50 percent of girls 15 to 19 had had sex. A separate but similar study found a 5-percentage-point drop as well among boys in that age group: 55 percent had experienced intercourse, compared with 60 percent in 1988.

The survey on girls also found that more of them were likely to use birth control the first time they had sex: three of four had used contraception the first time, compared with about 64 percent found doing so in surveys in the late 1980s. Much of the increase is due to more condom use, the new study found.

The Advice-Giver

Rachel

I'm the **advice-giver.** My best friend, Lilly, **likes me for me** not because I listen to her. Still many of my friends **are like my children** and I'm the mom. They know I even mother myself.

You see, my mom has never been able to do that for me. Starting when I was little, she was not the let-me-read-you-a-story type. Instead, I had to grow up fast. Even now we go out to dinner and it's not a Mom-and-Rachel dinnertime when I hear, "I'm always there for you." I don't want to be the adult all the time.

Most of us are fourteen. We have talks about everything, including who they hooked up with and what exactly happened. When it comes to sex "don't do it" is my usual advice, followed by "just think. If you have sex with this person, what does it prove? You're more a woman? You're more a man?"

A lot of my friends have sex for the same reason they might do drugs or alcohol. They're in the mood. "Even if you think everyone's doing it, that's no reason for you," I say. "Even if you're in love, sex and things like STDs and pregnancy that could go along with it are a Big Deal. Are you ready for any of that?"

Being a take-care person is both an escape and a burden. Helping friends keeps me from having to figure out my life. Lately, though, I don't want this role. Caleb, my own problem, weighs me down.

FLASHBACK

When I first notice Caleb, he's the perfect guy for me: popular and cute, a soccer player and an in-line skater. We go from friends to hanging out to that flirting-calling stage. "I stay in my room," I say. "I can't face my mom."

Even though Caleb has a life where things are more in place, he listens. "Spend the night at my house," he says. My parents trust me with that, and so do his. We're developing a closeness. I don't tell him "I love you," but we are definitely together.

Of course, Lilly and I talk, too. She has more to say than Caleb about my parents' separation and divorce. It's the middle of their horrible custody battle and I don't know where I stand in either parent's life.

Finally, I say to my mom, "I'm too depressed to live with you. I'll live with Dad." It breaks her heart. Caleb, Lilly and my other friends are mad and upset. My dad lives hours from here. Over and over they say, "You were always going to be there for us."

THE WORST PERSON

By my computer I have a wall of pictures of them all. When I read their e-mails, I can feel the distance. "Well, when are you coming home?" they write. I give them a date and then have to break it. I feel torn all the time. "You're the worst person in the world," one e-mails me. Does that mean we're not friends any more?

Meanwhile, though, my parents haven't finished their fights over me. On a Friday morning, we have to be in court where my mom lives. It's the same day as a big dance at the school I went to. All my friends are going. Caleb and I can go together. I'm excited about seeing him, but the court appearance is what's on my mind.

Caleb calls and after a while, he says, "If you're not going to be happy, don't go to the dance." I take what he says the wrong way. "He's angry with me?" I think. "Well, I'm angry at him." I call Sam, his best friend. Over the last few months we constantly talk about Caleb. In his own way, he's an advice-giver like me.

Once things calm down, it's decided: I stay at Lilly's. Caleb and I go to the dance. And that's what we do. By the end of the dance, everyone knows we're together. Still for all the tension and anxiety followed by Caleb's emotional support, there's none of that let's-have-sex talk. We're more about sweet kisses.

"Don't go back to your dad's," Caleb says. "It's sad here without you."

What can I do but cry.

I LOVE YOU

Saturday Caleb and I do those just-because things. Play basketball. Hang out. That night at the movies he buys me this beautiful 100% plastic gumball ring. "I love you" is written on it in red letters.

In the morning he comes to Lilly's to say goodbye. He takes me aside and says, "Rachel, I love you." A guy never told me that. I know that I really really like him, but I don't love him. I think, "I'm going to hurt him if I don't say it." At that moment, Lilly comes into the living room to tell Caleb his mom's on the phone. She needs to talk to him.

I whisper to Lilly what's going on. She says, "Just tell him you love him."

"But I don't."

As the days and weeks go by, I begin to realize I do love him. It isn't anything he says or a particular moment. I simply miss him so much.

Real love, I decide, is whatever you think it is. I love him the way you do at fourteen. Not the I'm-going-to-marry-him-and-have-children. More the girl liking the guy so much she feels the need to say, "I love you."

I call him up and say, "Caleb, I love you."

OUR ROUTINE

From then on Caleb and I try to see each other as often as we can manage. Once we plan that he and Sam will visit for the weekend. Instead, Caleb comes by himself. We decide to meet my friends here that he's talked to on the computer.

Of course, they love him. They say those chit-chat things, like, "Oh Rachel, you're meant to be with him."

But then Caleb and I know we want to be alone. It becomes our routine. We walk along the river, talking. It's intense and calming. I don't think about friends or family stress or school. He is my get-away. He jokes with me. He understands me. He says and does things that make me emotionally glow.

I start dream-date wondering, "Is Caleb the right guy at the right time? If we don't make love now, will it ever happen?" I feel the pressure.

MAD AT YOU

Then out of nowhere this Caleb thing turned into a mess. Suddenly Sam told me he was sick of hearing about Caleb. "What was that supposed to mean?" I wondered, until Caleb said, "Sam likes you and it hurts him."

I was stunned. I didn't know. And then it went totally weird. "Sam's mad at you; I'm mad at you, too," Caleb announced. Confused, I started thinking, Did I do something wrong? Did I just never realize how immature Caleb was?

Caleb seemed to get only angrier. I'd never had anybody I loved that much be so angry with me. Finally he wouldn't even talk. Lilly told me he was turning friends against me. I could never hate him, but I felt so upset that he talked behind my back and didn't talk to me.

From the weekend of the court date and the school dance to now was a year. That was a huge chunk of time. I sang along with lyrics like "...I wanna bathe with you in the sea. I wanna live life is forever until the sky falls down on me." I wrote poems in a font so tiny, I could write my heart out, but never be able to read it again.

Losing Caleb made me think about friends and question the way I felt about guys. "Was I too controlling?" I wondered, "Not there enough for Caleb?"

I sat at the computer and waited for him to sign on. I wanted to apologize. I sent him love letters on why I needed his friendship at least. In return, when he didn't ignore me, he sent messages hassling me about Sam. When he said, "No one here loves you," it sent me on a downward spiral. I didn't care about anything but Caleb. I had to block him from my mind. I had to mother myself and turn into my own advice-giver.

ABOUT ME

"Rachel," I say to myself. "I'm there for you. Caleb brings you too much pain. You have to live your life. It's time to get over him." "Rachel," I say to myself. "Nobody but you can tell you you're worthy. Even when it's hard, you have to love yourself."

"Rachel," I say to myself, "Maybe the lesson you're supposed to learn is that things change. Don't take back all the joy and pain your love for Caleb brought you. But for now your life has to be about you."

"And Rachel, despite the raging emotions, aren't you glad you never gave yourself to him? You trusted yourself to make the right choices at the right moments. And those moments will return when you are truly sure and ready."

June 19, 1994. The *New York Times*, Judith Newman.

Proud to Be a Virgin

A recent Sprecher-Regan study on 200 college virgins listed thirteen reasons why a person might want to remain a virgin. Both men and women rated "I haven't been in love or been in a relationship long enough" as the primary reason. Fears about pregnancy and AIDS were close behind.

On average, religious beliefs were seventh on the list of reasons for women, ninth for men. "Lack of sexual desire" was last on the list for both sexes, shattering the image of the virgin ice queen (or king).

Naked Alone Together

Pam

I'm **not** the **kind of girl** who can't go two days without **a boyfriend**. And I'm not searching for some guy because I **haven't seen my father since** I was a baby.

Still, I do have an ideal guy in mind. I want him to be responsible. That's important. In the looks department he's Matt Damon with Donald Trump's money, Albert Einstein's brains, James Dean's sensitivity. And he treats me good.

Last year there I was, waiting for the right guy to come along. With everybody always talking about how great sex was, it was hard to wait, but I was trying. I told myself being friends was a lot better than being lovers.

Then starting a few months ago, I began to think my world was falling apart. First, my friend Betsy moved to Florida. Next, my friend Annie's new boyfriend started beating her up. Worst of all, my friend Kelly got killed. I understood death comes to everyone, but not to fifteen-year-old girls with plans and dreams.

I stayed in my room and talked on the phone to my last good girlfriend, Tina. We told each other all our problems. She wrote poems for her pain, and my pain, too. She gave me copies.

Tina wrote one for Emily about her rotten boyfriend. She called it "Black and Blue."

When I showed it to my mom, she said, "Pam, go out. Make some new friends." So, I do.

BACKSEAT LOVE

I paint my fingernails black. I put on a striped T-shirt, my cargopants, and black leather Keds. I'm ready to head for P&B—Pocket and Billiards.

Right away I'm meeting all these people—Graham, Ronny, Alan, Maria. Some are from school. Some are older. Maria's an emancipated minor; she doesn't live with any parent. Afterward, we go to her apartment to party.

I spend the night there. When I tell my mom I'm staying at Maria's, she says, "Fine. Be home by eleven tomorrow morning." Mom has no idea what happens once I'm out the door.

I don't tell her that within a month I lose my virginity to Graham, one of those Cool Guys. On a Saturday morning he shows up at Maria's and says, "Want a ride home?"

"Sure," I say.

We drive around until he pulls into an elementary school parking lot. He says, "Let's be friends forever. Make love to me."

Maybe it's the emotional buildup. Curiosity. Timing. Mainly I'm thinking, Graham's not gonna like me unless I do it. "Yeah," I tell him, and we climb into the back seat of his GeoMetro.

I don't tell him I'm a virgin. Even if I did, I don't know if it would make any difference. I'm thinking, "Sex is going to be, like, real nice," stuff like that. Instead, I'm moaning not from pleasure, but from pain. There's even blood!

How can people keep doing it all the time, saying it's so fun, when it hurts? At least this first time. I guess it's different for somebody who's losing her virginity to a guy she really loves, not someone she just thinks she sort of cares about.

Fifteen minutes later, we're back in the front seat heading for my home. If you want to know the truth, I'm embarrassed about where it happened. I try not to think about Graham. I can tell we're only going to be see-ya-in-class friends. I'm right. Within two weeks we don't talk on the phone or go out or anything.

THE STERILE STORY

I've been told that you have to be honest with your feelings. I think I'm too open too quickly. I trust too much. Right away, everyone knows my strengths and my weaknesses. Ronny did.

Later I hear that Ronny calls himself the gigolo of P&B. The night I meet him, he's complaining that Irene, his ex, played him out through their whole relationship.

I know Irene from school. We've been friends. I don't know what to think.

He starts pressuring me. Lots of guys, when they're pressuring you, say, "Oh, I'm sterile." Ronny's not the one to tell me, Maria did. That's how I know it's true that he's sterile.

I don't think of asking him about protection. I don't think of STDs. I don't know how to say no. I just go ahead. The next day alone in my room, I read Tina's poem, "Naked Alone Together." She wrote it for me.

STD SCARE

My mom yells, "Irene's on the phone!"

"Not this past weekend, but the week before, I got chlamydia from Ronny," Irene says.

I hang up, scared. Why is she telling me this? Should I believe her? I know for a fact she slept with Graham, then Trippet before she slept with Ronny, then who knows who else. Maybe she got it from Trippet and gave it to Ronny?

I go to the county department of health for a checkup. They tell me I don't have chlamydia, but I do have an infection. It could be that Ronny cut my vagina wall and something about bacteria from my period.

All I hear is that I don't have chlamydia. I take the condoms they give me and leave.

PROMISE ME

Maria tells her boyfriend's best friend, Peter, to come over after P&B. I had told her I wanted to meet him. So he did, and we sat around, and one thing led to another. I don't have to tell you what.

"You have a perfect body," Peter says to me. He likes that my hair's natural, not pretend blond.

I sleep with him once, twice, three times. We talk about everything. He's real smart. He's working at Houlihan's to save money for college.

When I tell Tina about him, she writes "Hollow Promises."

I think of those words when Peter tells me, "We can't sleep together anymore."

"What?" I say.

"What you have going against you is your age."

"What's wrong with my age?"

He goes, "My age."

Peter's twenty and I'm fifteen. Of course I told my mom he's seventeen. On my way home I keep wishing I'd said something dramatic like, "Well, Peter, I still offer you my shoulder and my ear. I'll give you my opinion when you ask for it, my silence when you don't." But I didn't.

THREE GUYS TOO MANY

By the time I'm home, I break down. I try to make sense out of what I'm going through. Okay, I've slept with three different guys.

But everybody who hangs out at P&B has sex with each other at one time or another. Yet hardly anybody is even going out together, like boyfriend-girlfriend.

I don't think we should do that anymore. After you sleep with someone, you should be close. You should stay true.

I make a decision. I won't go out with guys purely for sex. I'll go out with them to see if they understand me or not. So far, it seems one guy's like the next. Maybe I'll just try to cover up my emotions.

My mom hears me crying and comes in my room. I tell her some of this stuff about my friends. I don't let her know I've been sexually active. "Maybe you're spending too much time caring about other people and not enough time caring about yourself," she says.

She gives me a hug.

I want my mom to meet someone who really loves her and she can really love. I know she wants to get married again. She'd like to share our split-level in suburbia.

That's what I'd like for both of us: Mom married and me in a steady relationship. But until that happens, at least I have a good mom and my sweet friend, Tina. No more casual sex for me.

What about Love

Frank

I wouldn't mind having **somebody to call my girl- friend.** I just don't want a relationship where I spend all my time. I've learned if you **get close** to people, **it hurts** a lot when they **walk away.**

CONVERSATION

My mom and dad have been in a cult since before I was born. Until I was nine, we lived together with the other members. Adults not good at anything like computing or accounting watched the children. One by one kids left the cult. When no adults were available to parent me, they'd leave me alone on the top floor of a warehouse. Finally, I moved to the suburbs to live with my grandmother.

Now seven years later I'm sixteen. I figure, if Gram and I weren't related, I'd hate her. She invades my life. When she saw my grades last report card, she said, "You can only stay out one night a weekend." My friends are always saying, "I haven't gone home for five days." Their parents care for them, but without the rules.

My Gram and I argue about everything. "Frank," she says, "I'm not worried. I only want to know what's on your mind." Imagine that nerve-wracking conversation.

"Well, Gram, I've been wondering about girls, the way they look and act. Will I ever have a date? And what about love? Is it a feeling inside you, like hunger or thirst? Something you think rather than know?"

My grandmother's the last person I'd want to analyze this stuff with. I'm a solitary person, anyway. When I'm with someone my age, I can talk. In crowds, forget it. Some kids at school and I never talk except on AOL. I compose my thoughts better on-line.

I'm trying to get into the guitar. I'm also studying its roots in history. When I play, the life around me vanishes. I spend most my free time doing homework, watching TV or practicing.

OVER?

Two years ago I had my first semi-serious crush. Andrew, a friend of mine, tried to hook me up with this girl, Denise. He said she had a huge crush on me. When I talked to her, I found out he'd told her the same thing about me. I didn't care. I liked her. I felt like asking her out.

I told Andrew and he turned around and told Denise! After that he came back to me with some story about a boyfriend that she planned to dump. "Uh, Frank," he said, "don't call her yet." A few days later his story was she's not dumping the boyfriend.

Last year in ninth grade, we had a class trip to New York City. I'd seen this girl, Caron, at parties and school. We hung out together the whole day while we went through museums. On the bus heading home, I still didn't know a lot about her, but the sadness in her eyes got me.

I was already thinking about going out with her. Then I noticed the silence. She stopped talking to me altogether. The next day in class she handed me a note and said, "Read this at lunchtime." As soon as she left the room, I read the message: "It's over." Over? It had barely started. I wanted to hook back up with her, but how could I act on it? I was angry, too. All I did, though, was go silent and feel the pain in my stomach.

When I told a friend what happened, he said it sounded like what I can't have, I want. I don't know.

ON-LINE LOVE

A month ago this girl, Molana, starts sending me AOL instant messages. "I'm intrigued by your profile," were the words in the box.

"I probably wouldn't have responded if you sent me e-mail," I reply back.

We discover we're both in the same grade. We both go to private schools. She likes seventies music. "I just got two CDs, a Jimi Hendrix and a Santana," I write her.

I know a bunch of kids who do drugs, but I don't. "I'm the same way," she says. I tell her I found out from a student that I can look like a drug burnout. "Maybe that's why most teachers don't like me," I say.

"I was wondering how you look," she replies.

"I'm not ugly, but I'm not like Prince Charming. What about you?"

"I'm five feet six in the punk-preppy realm."

"I'm over six feet, not skinny, not fat. And I work out."

"You ought to know, I'm not into action flicks," Molana writes.

"You sound like a cute, straight-A student," I write back, "Is it time to see each other in person?"

"What about this Friday?"

"I'm in a play this weekend so that won't work. How's next week Saturday?"

"Great. Where, when and what will you be wearing?"

"...I guess jeans with a black T-shirt and Nikes."

"Cool."

I didn't ask what she'd be wearing. I'm not that curious. I've just decided I'm willing to take another change. I still want a girlfriend, even though I feel stronger. I'm independent I've been making friends. Now that my nonexistent love life doesn't bother me, maybe I'll have one.

FLOATING

I think about who I'd be if my parents had left the cult when I was born. I know I'd be a different person. Maybe even a happier person. I wonder if my mom's feeling depressed. I haven't talked to my dad in years, but twice this year, she stopped by. That's a record.

My experience with and without them has taught me this: I have to make sure I have someone or something to hold onto. Since no parents are around for me, I have to look for any solid adult—even a grandmother—a girlfriend, or what's best in my case, a guitar. Before I started to play I didn't how depressed I was.

I didn't think I was good at anything and I wasn't getting anywhere in life. That's one of the worst feelings to have. The guitar became something to reach for instead of treading water in the middle of the ocean.

Maybe other teenagers should try to find that one thing to keep you floating.

November 1998. *The Brown University Child and Adolescent Behavior Letter,* John J. Colby, Ph.D.

Substance Abuse

Well-to-do suburban kids are the most likely teenagers to use alcohol and marijuana, according to recent reports. Those kids are often involved in athletics and other school activities and typically do well in their studies and appear to be happy and well adjusted. Their drug use, especially their tendency to binge drink, belies their otherwise normal development. For most affluent high school kids, using some drugs, especially alcohol, is the norm, not the exception. When asked, "Why do you drink a lot?" well-to-do teenagers are likely to say, "Why not?"

Parents Fail to Challenge Teen Thinking

Seeing no reason not to binge drink at parties and before school suggests that well-to-do teenagers have not been challenged to think about what is healthy and responsible. Research indicates that assumption is correct. And not talking about responsible health behavior is made worse when parents believe that teenage drinking is okay, even expected. Conversely, when parents set clear rules about drinking, talk with their teenagers about their concerns, and monitor friends and activities, the most dangerous patterns of drinking are prevented.

Love on the Run

Kirsten

WHILE RIP WATCHED THE KIDS, ME AND CURTIS SAT ON THE PORCH AND TALKED. WE DIDN'T REALLY LOOK AT EACH OTHER AT FIRST. BUT THEN WE GOT COMFORTABLE. I LIKED HIM BECAUSE HE ASKED ABOUT ME. AFTER A WHILE WE EVEN HELD HANDS.

WHAT MUSIC DO YOU LIKE?

HEAVY RAP AND ROCK.

WE GO TO CANFIELD'S TO DANCE AND HANG.

I DON'T LIKE RAP.

WHAT'S YOUR FAVORITE COLOR AND FOOD?

BLACK AND LASAGNA

THAT'S A NEAT JACKET.

WE ALWAYS WEAR FLIGHT JACKETS.

WHO'S "WE"?

A WOMAN FOUND ME AND TOOK ME TO THE HOSPITAL. I WAS BLEEDING REAL BAD. THEY SAID I LOST THE BABY.

THEN MY MOM AND DAD WERE, LIKE, "WE'RE SORRY, KIRSTEN." BUT I HAD HATE IN ME.

Declaration of Independence

Ofelia

When I was a kid,
I thought one day
Prince Charming
would show up. We'd
fall **madly in love.**
All my problems would
go away. We'd live
**happily ever
after.** Sure. I woke
up. I stopped looking.
Prince who?

I didn't think about Antoine that way. He just happened.

I had known him a long time. We talked together. I don't remember why, but we began calling each other, too. Finally he said, "Enough of this playing around. Do you like me?"

I said, "I'd like to get to know you better."

That was the start. I wanted to make sure I had strong feelings for him; and it wasn't just my physical emotions taking over.

After awhile I decided I did have feelings. I wasn't in love with the idea of love. I knew it was a big responsibility to have a relationship that included sex. Still, I was seventeen. I was ready to be with Antoine.

Once I made that decision, it was hard to keep it to myself. I thought, "How am I going to go about actually having sex with him? Do I sneak away? Do I tell my mom?"

My mom barely tolerated him. She kept hoping he'd disappear from the picture. Antoine came from a poor family. He was used to being out in the street.

I've always had a sheltered life. My family's very protective. Whatever I need, I get. I don't know what it's like to be out at all hours. That's exciting to me.

What my mom sees is that Antoine's African-American. What I see is an outgoing, good-looking guy. You want to be around him. He's not the kind to fall into the locker-room trap. You know, the boys who talk about how they scored.

On the other side, Antoine's family is prejudiced against white people. He admits they're not happy about my skin color, and that's just part of the problem.

Antoine is able-bodied. I think of myself as differently abled. For ten years I've been partially paralyzed and had nerve problems because of an automobile accident. I use a wheelchair.

Antoine's family is always asking him, "Why would you want a girl like that?"

He tells them, "It doesn't bother me." His favorite cousin uses a chair. It's not a mystery for him. Until this year I feared rejection. I was self-conscious about my body to begin with.

I worried, "Maybe the chair will be such a turn-off, he'll never see past it." But Antoine saw me, the person, and not the chair. Anyway, I have a pretty great personality.

LOVE PLANS

Privacy is a problem for us. Antoine's family lives on the tenth floor in an apartment building. The elevator is usually broken. I live in a two-story house with my mom, my two sisters, my aunt, my uncle, and three cousins. My father died when I was an infant.

I can't do a lot of intimate things for myself. I need home attendants to help me. None of them stays too long. There are always different people doing different things for me.

My mom has power over me, more than most teenagers have to cope with. She can be intimidating. When I was little, I idolized her. Now I know she's human.

Antoine and I started planning how we could be together. We decided, first things first: What are the different kinds of contraception, and which ones are best for us? With my disability, what are my limitations on how my hands work?

I went to Planned Parenthood. I told the counselor, "My boyfriend and I are thinking about using condoms and the foam."

"Will you be able to manipulate the spermicide applicator?" the counselor asked.

"No," I said. "I can't use my hands enough to put in a diaphragm or push the foam applicator. It's okay, though. My boyfriend says he'll do it."

She said, "Good for you. Some young women would never dream of asking their partner to put in the diaphragm."

"You mean girls are going to do something so personal and intimate with a guy, but they can't talk about contraception with him?"

"Surprising, huh?" the counselor said.

Of course, Planned Parenthood was easy compared to telling my mother. I remember that conversation like it was yesterday. What came out was, "Mom, Antoine wants to be with me."

Her eyes became slits. She's thinking, "This black guy is going to take my baby away." I'm embarrassed to even be talking to my mom about this stuff.

I'm thinking, "I could have phrased it better."

"I knew this was going to come up," she says. "Ofelia, why can't you wait?"

I agree. I want to wait anyway.

COMPLETELY ALONE

I always thought the first time I make love, it will be so romantic. For us, it's more like a schoolbook comedy.

We figure out we can do it in a hotel. We look through the Yellow Pages to call places to compare the price. After we pick a hotel, Antoine says, "It's not close to public transportation. How should we get there?"

"We could rent a van," I say. We call an ambulette service to see how much that would cost. We can afford it, so we say, "Okay."

I'm packing a bag when the phone rings and the ambulette people say, "The van broke down. Can we send a car?"

We don't know what to do. Because of my paralysis, I can't

sit up well without support. Antoine says, "I have to learn to put you in and out of a car. I'll start with this." I don't know how much I weigh, but I'm no lightweight.

I'm falling for Antoine more each day.

The driver gets here, and he only speaks Spanish. I speak some Spanish, but I don't know how to get to the hotel. Just as we're calling another car, my mom comes home!

She knows where we're going. And she doesn't want to be here to see us actually drive away. She leaves. I feel awful.

I'm not nervous—until we get there. I look back at it now and I realize the hotel was a dump. But that day Antoine put me at ease.

We get in the room, and all I can see is the bed.

My heart starts beating.

Antoine turns on the TV.

We're completely alone.

That has never happened before. Someone is always in and out of my house. The instant he starts putting me in the bed, it flashes through my mind, "I don't want to be here." I don't say anything.

Antoine is good. He doesn't push me. Still, sex is not wonderful. Since I can't walk, the hymen never stretches. His penis inside me really hurts. Afterward I'm, like, that's it? I try to hide from Antoine that it takes so long before the hurt goes away.

He asks me, "How was it? Tell the truth."

"Well, it was not what I expected," I say.

We leave on a Friday afternoon and come back Sunday. We walk in the door, and there's my mother. I keep thinking that she's thinking about Antoine and me together. I can't look at her. This is the woman who gave birth to me and raised me, and she doesn't approve.

TOMORROW

Antoine and I have been together two years now. Sometimes it's hard to say whether a boyfriend's worth it. There have been a lot of tissues and tears. Because I never have much privacy, we have to sneak around to be together. That takes its toll. For all the pain with Antoine, he's also helped me realize there are things I can handle on my own.

He's always encouraged me to explore my neighborhood. I remember the first time I went to the park by myself. It's four scary blocks away. It felt good. I told some friends, and they were shocked I went by myself.

Before Antoine, I would never have dreamed about having my own apartment. I was terrified of being alone. I was so dependent on my mother. Now I form my own opinions. I'm getting anxious to move out. I've applied to a place, only I haven't told my mom yet.

I'd like Antoine to be in my future. It's shaky right now. He comes to see me practically every day. He says, "It bothers me that you won't tell your mother you're not happy with the way things are."

When he says that, I get angry with myself. Now, though, it's a healthier anger. I direct my anger in positive ways. I went by a store that was being remodeled. It's three floors and has no elevator. Who's going to carry me and my chair up the stairs?

I ask the manager, and he says, "Oh, we're going to put in an elevator soon."

I went back, and there still wasn't one. I think, "Should I make a case about it?" I'd like to be an activist, and partly I have Antoine to thank for that.

Maybe he's today's Prince Charming. Antoine has helped

me figure out who I am and what my beliefs are. He's helped me explore my feelings and begin to be independent. And he's helped me be just like any other teenager.

Dear Janet,

Two years ago, I lost my boyfriend, Malik. He had just turned to me and said, "I have never been this happy. I love you!" At that moment my brother came into the room playing with my dad's shotgun. Blam. In a blink he shot Malik. He was not moving with his blood and other stuff, I guess, from the brain) covering me.

Malik and my brother were close as kin. While he showed his pain, I kept mine inside. Everyone forgot about me and concentrated on him. He kept saying couldn't live knowing what he did. He wanted to kill himself. By that first night my brother was in a mental hospital.

A clean-up crew came to our house and took anything contaminated with Malik's blood. I managed to sneak away a blood-drenched bunny he'd given me. To this day I can't wash it. I'd feel I was washing away the only part I have left of him.

Months passed and then there was a trial. I loved his family, but when

Malik died they turned me into the enemy. I had to go in front of a judge, his family and tons of other people. Step by step, detail by detail, in between my tears I had to tell the sequence of events that horrible day.

My brother's been in jail and he's due out soon. Even now he's the one my parents pay attention to. They've forgotten I was there, too. I feel I'm a victim of what happened, just like Malik was. Not my brother, he is not the victim. I don't hate my brother, but because of him my life will never be the same.

Thinking back, it would have helped if I had a place to visit Malik, but he was cremated. I grieve in the privacy of my room. It's covered with things that have to do with him. On my wall I have a huge picture of him. I have angels all over, because Malik means "angel" in Arabic. Not one guy can handle being second and knowing that my room is a memorial.

Oh, Malik I will always love you.

LaDonna

Seth

I live in a laid-back **suburb** of New York City. My **parents** are politically liberal and **morally conservative.** They're **raising me** on marriage, children, and family. They're very **strict.**

It's clear they don't want me growing up too fast. And in this quiet town, they're afraid of what might be going on after midnight, from drugs to violence to running with the wrong crowd.

But I have a different problem. I just didn't realize it until this year.

To get me away from their fears, the summer before tenth grade, they sent me to a Mediterranean sailing camp. That's where I met my first girlfriend, Heather.

She was a cool blonde who wore cool clothes, my ideal at the time. I was terrified she wouldn't think I was good enough for her. I was naive. Heather was aggressive. We did a lot of things, but I didn't want to have sex.

I was embarrassed to be naked in front of anyone. I didn't feel ugly; I felt awkward. What Heather and I did was always under the covers.

By the time I got home, though, I knew I wanted a social life. I didn't want to be popular. I just wanted to be with the people in my class who looked like they were having a good time.

Every step of the way has become a battle. The first time I asked to go to a party, my parents wanted to drive me there and pick me up at ten o'clock—their curfew for me!

I'd do anything to get out. Lie. Sneak. Pretend things. They started putting me on more restrictions. They wanted to know every move I was making. I began to stay over at friends'.

We were into drinking, drugs, and trips to the city. We became regulars at one club in particular and would get passes to come back each time we went. I'd leave home in jeans and a T-shirt. In my bag I had my club gear ready to go.

The one night I came home smelling of alcohol, my mother said, "Seth, you're going to a therapist."

The therapist said, "Do you have a drinking problem?"

I said, "I go out on Friday night and have a beer. Is that a problem?" I didn't tell him I was starting to fall in love with a guy. It happened before I knew it.

NOVEMBER

We've been friends a couple of years. This year we have a lot of classes together. We go to the same parties.

If you ask me what I like about him, I'd say, "Everything." He seems secure in his life. I'm in constant turmoil. We have the same interests. We even dress similarly.

He's good-looking. Other people like him. His name is Zach, and he's on my mind all the time. I wonder, "Why is this happening?"

I'm angry. I don't want to be gay. And more than anything, I don't want anybody to know. Not Zach, either. I pray he doesn't feel the same way. I don't know what's going to happen if he does.

The idea of a gay relationship upsets and depresses me. I spend hours in my room doing nothing but listening to why-does-God-hate-me music. My life is a mistake.

I don't look in the phone directory for a gay hotline or support group. I don't want to deal with it. I want those feelings to go away.

One afternoon, I do some research in the library. I look up homosexuality in the encyclopedia. Most of what I read is technical. I want to know, can I do anything to change my feelings?

I'm afraid the only cure I'll read about is some therapist zapping a gay man with a cattle prod while showing him pictures of men together.

Are people born gay or is it in the raising? I read both arguments. A girl I know comes up and says, "Hey, what are you reading?" I hide the page.

There are about six hundred students in our high school. To be openly gay isn't tolerated. You'd be targets of the jocks and the kind who throw bottles at the school on weekends. You could be in physical danger.

One night after I've been in a school play, some guys corner me. They push me around. They call me faggot. They don't know, it's just an expression. But it scares me.

A girl I know stands around laughing. She seems to enjoy seeing me get into trouble. Teens are cruel to begin with. I had negative feelings about gays, too.

My parents say, "As long as gays stay in Greenwich Village and don't bother anybody, they can do what they want. Well, almost anything. We don't want to see them on the street having a parade. And we don't want to see them teaching our kids at school."

All I know about gays is they are supposed to be into casual sex. That's opposite of how I feel. All I want is to be so emotionally attached that eventually we sleep together.

I go into the city by myself, and somebody's put a tremendous sign in front of Grand Central Station: AIDS IS THE WRATH OF GOD ON ALL HOMOSEXUALS. ALL HOMOSEXUALS MUST DIE.

DECEMBER-FEBRUARY

Some days at school, I don't think I'm going to make it through. I feel I'm falling off the edge. On weekends I get up at four in the afternoon.

It's harder and harder to pretend I only think of Zach as a friend. We spend time together, and when I leave, I'm barely out the door before I'm crying about it.

I can't keep it inside. A bunch of us are at a party. I say to my friend Wendy, there's something I want to tell you, but I'm afraid it might change how you think of me.

"You can trust me," she says.

"I'm attracted to Zach."

"It's obvious."

"Do you think he might be gay?"

"I'm pretty sure he's not. I'm not saying you shouldn't be gay, but your attraction to Zach is not going to work. It's just trouble for you."

Wendy has had lots of relationships. She knows how these things work. She says, "Give yourself time. You won't feel as bad as you do right now."

I don't believe her. I do feel relief, though. I've spoken the words: I'm attracted to Zach.

"If you keep sitting in your room, mulling it over, crying, it's going to get worse," she says. "Find someone else."

By chance, telling Wendy lets out my secret. Another good friend, Andrea, overheard our conversation. She joins in, "Zach's been wondering what's going on. You have to talk to him. If you ignore it, you're going to ruin your friendship."

I run the idea of sex with a man through my head. I'm affectionate. But I don't know how to get beyond that. Even with Zach, the fantasy isn't about great sex. I want to be with him. I want to have a sharing, caring relationship.

I'm depressed.

MARCH-

MAY

We're at a party where finally I confront Zach. I get drunk. We leave together, but we're going in opposite directions. Before saying good-bye, I tell him, "I'm sorry to do this, but there's something I need to talk to you about."

I have spent hours figuring out how to tell him. I'm prepared for the answer. I see two possibilities: He feels the same way. Or he's horrified.

I'm frightened.

I don't think he'll be nasty. But saying anything to him could hurt our friendship. What if he does feel the same way? I don't understand anything about being gay.

Finally I say it: "Zach, I'm attracted to you."

He answers right away. "Oh, that's okay," he says, "It doesn't bother me."

It doesn't bother him! What's that supposed to mean? He likes me? He hates me? He wants to be anywhere but having this conversation? Is he surprised? Will this change our friendship? Is he telling the truth?

I can't believe it. I didn't anticipate that answer. It leaves too many doors open. I can't bring myself to say, "Well, do you think you're gay? Even if you are, you aren't attracted to me?"

I go through this whole buildup, and I get an ambiguous answer. I'm almost angry. For the million things I want to say, all I can manage is "I'm sorry."

"There's nothing to be sorry about," Zach says. And then we say goodnight.

I'm so late coming home, my mother's waiting for me. She starts to search me. She's suspicious of drugs. My father comes downstairs and is lecturing me on being rude to my mother, when she finds my cigarettes.

They're furious. To them, smoking is a dirty habit. Only someone who hates himself smokes. I run past them to my room. I'm sure they're thinking, "What a troubled young man." It's always my troubles. They never see that they're involved.

I want them to go to family counseling. My father refuses, and my mother sends me instead. I'm sixteen years old and already I'm on my second therapist.

This one isn't any better than the first one. There I am with a bearded, forty-five-year-old pipe-smoking man. He's going to listen to my sexual problems? He talks about the different stages of a child and asks about my sexual fantasies.

SEPTEMBER

After that conversation, Zach pretends it never happened. I'm convinced he hates me. Still, I feel a little better since my feelings are no longer a complete secret. The obsession, though, is worse. To relieve the tension, I get stoned coming and going to school. My life seems hopeless.

I'm so unhappy day-to-day, I try to believe there will be some sort of justice in the future. Nobody should go through this for no reason.

My parents send me to Atlanta for the summer to stay with my aunt and uncle. I still have not touched a guy. I haven't done much more with a girl.

Within a couple weeks of going to Georgia, I meet this girl, Stephanie. We become friends. One afternoon, she bleaches my hair. We get drunk and have sex.

Emotionally I'm glad to get that over with. But I realize I'm not cut out to have relationships like that with a girl. We decide not to do it anymore.

I don't know if she puts two and two together, but that same day she introduces me to Josh.

95

Josh and I go out and then come back to his home. Everybody is gone. I kind of let sex happen. I'm curious. I need someone to push the issue, to say, "Let's try this."

Afterward, I go back to my aunt and uncle's and take a two-hour shower. Until now I haven't really dealt with being gay. My experience with Josh tells me I not only have to accept my homosexuality, I have to accept what gay sex is: the actual physical contact and what it means.

I'm tired of being angry with myself. Instead, I want to be honest. I tell myself, "Even if I can't tell other people the truth about me, I have to make sure I know what the truth is. The fact is, for now, to survive, I have to be pretty closeted."

But that makes me angry all over again. I wish I could tell straight teenagers: Don't judge other people. Gay and lesbian teens are no worse... and no better... than you are.

You may fear us. You may hate us. But don't turn those into action: Don't beat us. Don't persecute us. Don't take the time to worry about us. If nothing else, leave us alone.

It's easy to say, "No one close to me is homosexual." Well, do you really know what goes on in everyone's heart?

After vacation I know I have to convince myself and Zach that my feelings for him aren't serious anymore. I want to talk to him. Keep the friendship going.

Maybe we can talk about how we had so much in common. I saw a lot in him I wanted to be. I'll bring it up that way. I'll never use the word love. I'll never say why I felt the way I did.

"Don't worry," I'll say. "It was a supercrush, and it's over."

May 18, 1999. The *New York Times*, Nancy Beth Jackson.

From Gay Teenagers, a Cry for Help

Teenagers who are gay or bisexual are more than three times as likely to attempt suicide as other youth, according to a Massachusetts study reported this month. Young men are at particular risk, the report found. The lead researcher also noted these young people were more likely to engage in other high risk behaviors.

The Pre-Sex Inventory

Suki

I took **God in my life** when I was six. Now I'm eighteen. I'm still **religious**, just not super-religious. I don't like this idea that if you're not Christian, you're **going to hell.** I pray on my own. I listen to God, not preachers.

God helps me get through my time at home. My dad's on drugs. My mom mostly ignores me. She sleeps the morning away and then goes shopping or out with the girls. She says to me, you stupid this, you lazy that.

I don't say what I'm thinking. I can't talk to my mother about anything, let alone sex. I feel like an outcast.

When I was little, my grandmother was my caretaker. She'd help me with my cereal. Walk me to school. I knew my grandmother loved me. Each year for my birthday, she made me these lace dolls.

I turned a lot of my attention to school. I have awards that say I'm motivated. I plan to go to college.

In my neighborhood, your morals are important until you reach a certain age. Then everything changes. I could see how the older girls carry themselves. Most end up having sex by my age.

AFTERNOON RAPE

I met Jeff two summers ago, when I was feeling lousy. It was summer, and we'd hang out together. It was nice to get attention.

One afternoon he came over; no one else was home. I had my T-shirt on. When he realized I wasn't wearing a bra, he said, "I'm in the mood." He started doing things. He said he wanted to eat me for his Memorial Day picnic.

I was taken by surprise. I told him no. I was a virgin. He said, "Are you sure?" I was insulted.

"I thought you were nice," I said. "I thought you respected me."

He didn't care what I said. He was pushing me. I was saying, "No! I don't want to do this." He grabbed me, ripped off my shorts, and started jamming me everywhere. I thought my insides were going to fall out.

I was in such pain and bleeding. Afterward, he gave me a rag and said, "Go, clean up."

I took it, and as I got off the couch, the trail of blood started following me. When I stopped, it dripped down my leg and pooled on the floor. "Get out," I said. "You're just using and confusing me." With that, he left.

I went into my bedroom, and I said to myself, "Look what happened. I must be a slut. I don't deserve nice things."

I started to destroy things that meant a lot to me: the lace dolls my grandmother made, my awards from school. I heard myself say, "I wish I wasn't alive." I picked up a piece of broken glass to cut myself, but I didn't do it.

Instead, I whispered the words, "Suki, you are still a virgin. You were raped and that has nothing to do with choice, love or sex."

THE HURT

Now it's two years later. A guy named Robin is in my life. He's talented. He writes for the school newspaper. He wants to work directing and writing commercials.

He knows that I go through all sorts of things at home. If I start to go nuts, he grabs my hand. I realize I like hanging out with him. But he's shorter than me, and his features aren't what most people call handsome. I'm not ready to admit I'm attracted.

I say, "What would we do if we started dating each other?"

He says, "If you have to ask, forget it. The last thing I want to do is add pressure to your life."

"Well, who says you will?" I answer. "Let's try it."

The next time I see him, he gives me a quick kiss and a hug. I don't respond. I still think, "It isn't going to work. Why bother?"

But then we keep talking, watching TV, stuff like that. We talk about kids. For him, no boys, he only wants daddy's little girls to deal with. We wonder if we had kids, what would they be like? Gorgeous? Smart? As caring as I feel I am?

One day Robin says, "How do you feel about me?"

"I am kind of falling for you."

Then I lean over and give him a full kiss. I say, "I did this? Yikes! What does this mean?"

"You tell me," he says, meaning I'm the one who started things.

I say, "You're not seeing anyone else, are you?"

"No, are you?"

"No."

"Are we exclusive?" he says.

I give him a mile-long smile and say, "I guess it means we're boyfriend and girlfriend." I start to tell him my secrets.

We also talk about religion. I say, "I'm supposed to be a virgin when I get married."

Robin says, "You're going to listen to a book instead of your emotions?" I admit that sometimes I battle with religion.

For example, marriages are supposed to be blessed. Well, if they are, how come there's so much divorce? Maybe if you respect the person you're with, if you totally love him, it's okay to have sex if you're planning to stay together. Or is it?

I think about getting married. I'll find a nice dress, not a wedding dress. And it can be whatever color I choose. It depends on what mood I'm in; it might be something subtle or off the shoulder, with a piece of jewelry. I want flowers in my hair, and I'll wear it up.

I'd be very selective about who would come. Robin's family, even though his mother left when he was four and just came back into his life this year. He let her know, "You may be my mother, but don't tell me what to do." I'd invite my grandmother. I don't know about my parents.

NO PIECE OF MEAT

Robin doesn't feel that sex outside of marriage is a sin. Sometimes I agree with him. Other times I don't know. To me, it's important to be a virgin.

It would be great to have parents to talk to about sexual feelings. But I don't. I decide, though, I shouldn't ask a friend who's sexually active for advice. She'd tell me, "Yeah, do it."

I should try to talk to an adult. Then it's still up to me to decide whether that person makes sense. To get started, to help me think, I make an inventory.

This way I won't get caught unable to explain myself to Robin or any guy who pressures me. I don't want to ever be in a situation again like I was with Jeff.

Here's what I write.

1 *It will only give me heartache if I have sex just because:*
- Robin asks me
- I want to prove my love
- I'll feel like less of a person if I don't

Then I go on to my next part. I imagine why Robin wants to sleep with me. I add to my checklist.

2 *Robin wants to have sex because:*
- he loves me
- I'm physically attractive
- he's horny

103

3 *Where does he want to do it?*
- a parked car
- his house/my house
- a motel

4 *What problems can happen?*
- sexually transmitted diseases
- the condom breaks
- it will hurt because I'm totally nervous
- pregnancy!

I know some girls sleep with a guy and do certain things that the guy wants when they don't really want to. If I'm not sure whether I want to do something, I shouldn't let Robin talk me into it.

I also know girls who have sex because they've had sex before with another guy. They're a piece of meat for the latest one to dine on. I don't want to be like that. If I'm not ready for sex, I shouldn't do it.

I can't forget AIDS. Even though I think I know everything about Robin, maybe I don't. I should find out as much as I can. If I compromise, sleep with him, and then decide I made a mistake, I'll tell him, "Let's take a step back and not have sex again."

If he says no, then he's not worth it. And he shouldn't be questioning me as to why, unless he's doing it in an inquisitive way and not in a hey-we-already-did-it, it-doesn't-matter-anymore way.

LOVE TRUST

It's eleven months that Robin and I have been together. We do things that are physical but not quite sexual. Like, he'll kiss me and rub my stomach.

One time he stopped touching my body. He went downstairs and got some sodas. When he came back up, I said, "What's wrong?"

He said, "I know you're not ready to go further. I was getting excited. I didn't want anything to happen that shouldn't happen."

Now, though, he feels I don't trust him as much as I should. He feels he's proven himself, which is true. He says, "I'm not pressuring you, but can't you be more relaxed and uninhibited?" At first I wouldn't even close my eyes. He says, "Closing your eyes helps you block things out." Now I do it for a couple seconds at a time.

Still he knows I hold back. He wants me to take the initiative, do as I feel, not wait for him to make the moves. I try that, and it sort of works. I can give the first kiss, but I won't stick my tongue in his mouth or anything like that. I'd rather let him put his tongue in mine and then respond to him.

ONE HUNDRED PERCENT SURE

Robin lets me know that while he'll wait for me, he doesn't have to like it. He wishes we could make love. "Your religion is holding you back," he says.

"Maybe yes, maybe no," I tell him. "But I'm the one who has to control my sexual feelings, my body, and my life. I've prayed to God about it. For now, I still want to be more than one hundred percent sure before I give up my virginity."

And he says, "Okay, for now."

Controlling the Monster

Elizabeth

"Let's go to Lucy's to **watch the fireworks,"** says Andrew. The Fourth of July is my favorite holiday, and he knows it.

"Great," I say. Andrew and I have been **sort of together** for nearly a year.

He's exciting, sexually mature and brilliant. All the girls are after him. I make up conversations in my head where I tell him, "Some day you'll be head-over-heels in love with me. We'll have a forever connection, a place of our own. We can rent movies, order take-out, and just sit around." Instead, he breaks my heart so many times.

It's hot out that day. Andrew takes off his shirt and is strutting through the crowd feet ahead of me. I'm, like, "Helloooo."

He yells back at me, "I need a beer," and disappears into a bar. Within minutes he's drinking pitchers by himself.

"You show no concern for me," I say.

"So what? Other times I'm all over you." And with that he starts feeling me up in front of a bar full of people. I'm embarrassed and angry. I push him away.

"I'm going to Lucy's party," he says. "Take it or leave it."

"You're on your own," I say, and storm out the door.

There I am walking the streets, feeling alone. This always seems to happen. I'm, like, "I'm leaving him for good!" But where am I going to go? Not home, for sure. That's boring. I love my parents, but they're caught up in their own lives. My older brother, Mr. Perfect, doesn't have time for me, either.

When Andrew first really hassled me, I told my parents about it. My dad went over to his house and yelled at him. He said, "How could you hurt my daughter?"

He respects my dad. I thought, "Andrew's so upset, maybe now if we get back together, the screaming will be over." And it was, for awhile.

THE ULTIMATE CRIME

I start missing Andrew. I figure I'll go to Lucy's and find him.

By the time I get to her house, the party's taken over. I go upstairs and knock on a couple of doors. Nobody answers. I walk into a bedroom and there's—Andrew! He's with this girl Marilyn. She's fully clothed, and he's in his boxers. She's straddling him. I'm devastated. The ultimate crime in front of my eyes. "Get out of here!" he screams at me.

"I hate you, Andrew! You, too, Marilyn," I say while I'm crying and running down the stairs. "And Marilyn, I don't want to hate you. Before this I liked you."

Andrew yells after me, "You bring out the worst in me." Next thing I know, he's half-dressed, chasing me down the street. People we don't know threaten to call the police.

Andrew's scary when he's drunk. But I kind of find it—not exciting, but sort of like an adventure. We're both these crazy rebels. "We need to discuss what's going on," I tell him.

"We know what's going on. If you showed me more affection, I wouldn't turn to others, like Marilyn."

"But sometimes I just want us to hang out," I say. "I don't want to have sex."

"Sex means love," he says.

That stops me. "I know you always tell me your parents deprived you of love and attention when you were little."

"Yeah," he says, "and you're doing more of the same."

He starts to croon, "Oh, sweetie, I'm so lucky. I can't believe I have you in my life." He yells at me, and then he wants to hold me, treat me like a baby.

Finally he says, "I swear to God, Elizabeth. I'll never scream at you again."

CONTROL?

The next day, when Andrew's sober, I ask him, "What is going through your mind when you're treating me like that?"

He only focuses on the screaming, not on a reason behind it. He says, "When you're screaming at someone, you don't think and plan it."

"If the screaming just comes, it's like a monster that takes you over. It's the same as being high. And I don't think any guy can say, 'I'll never do it again' without some kind of help. You're not in control of it. It's controlling you."

"The only thing that's controlling me is you," he says, as he picks up my address book. He crosses out names and then rips up the pages. "Now I have a little control back over you," he says. "Those people are out of your life." In case I miss his point, he holds an umbrella at my neck. Then he laughs.

I'm in shock.

His mom comes into the room, and I say, "Your son has problems that need to be resolved." She's, like, from outer space. All she says is, "Don't go blaming your problems on my Andrew."

"Forget it," I say. "We're over."

"You'll be back," he says, when I walk out the door for the zillionth time.

THE COMMITMENT

This time is different. I go out with a guy named Hank. He goes to another school. Hank keeps saying, "Elizabeth, you're wonderful. You're beautiful."

"What fun," I think. When Andrew hears I'm seeing somebody, he's shocked. I've always been accessible to him. He's had me no matter what. After I tell him, "Hank gave me my first orgasm ever," overnight he changes. Andrew gets obsessed with me.

He shows up at our back door, drunk, demanding a commitment.

"Me being committed to you and you not being committed to me?" I say. "Is that what you mean? What about all those girls?"

"They were revenge. You and me, we're meant for each other."

He hasn't said "I love you," but he's close to it.

"I want to share something with you. I want you to have my baby," he says.

I'm thinking, "Come on, Andrew, say it, say it, tell me you love me."

"I lub you, Elizabeth."

Yes!

NO-WIN SITUATION

I decide to really pay attention to the things that upset Andrew. If I see what I do to trigger a bad response in him, I can stop doing it. Our problems will be over.

One Sunday we're at my house. My parents are gone for the weekend. He says, "Make me a couple of sandwiches." I go into the kitchen, make two, and bring them back to my room.

The screaming starts. "There's too much fat and not enough calories in them!" I'm supposed to remember he's body-building.

I'm wearing this ballerina pin my mom and dad gave me the Christmas I turned five. It seems to symbolize when I was younger and life was safe.

Andrew tears the pin off my shirt and smashes it with his fist. I spit on him. He punches me in the arm. Right then, my mom calls to see how I am. "Oh, fine," I say.

After I hang up, I think, "If I'm ever a mother, I don't want my daughter to say she's fine when she's in danger." There are times I'm in a corner crying, I picture being in my parents' arms. By now, they hate him. They know I'd only sneak if they forbid me from seeing him. They'd like to, though. I feel I'm a burden to them. All we talk about is Andrew.

A PASSIVE LIFE

Before Andrew, I collected a lot of friends. They labeled me confident. I pictured myself as leading the crowd, making others feel at ease. Now I only socialize with him and his friends. They don't see him as a brute and me as a victim. They think, "Elizabeth agitates Andrew. How could anyone put up with her?"

Is there something wrong with me? Do I have a temper, like Andrew says? I feel he's isolated me. When I'm not with him, I live in this little planet, my room. I keep my shades down. When I talk, I stumble over words. I'm not sure of myself. I'm not a leader. I'm not a follower.

I'm passive.

How can I leave him? I'd be too lonely. If I got together with one of my old friends, what would we do? Go to the movies? Anyway, the whole time I'd wish I was with Andrew.

I want to be with him because it's what I want to do.

I don't have anywhere to go if I'm not with him.

I love him. And supposedly he loves me.

The phone rings, and it's such a part of my life, even though I know I shouldn't answer it, I pick it up. Then it's impossible for me to hang up on him.

Sure, maybe he's extremely selfish. But people in general are selfish. They're into themselves. Andrew pays a lot of attention to me, and I can't get past that situation.

Still, there are more instances where I tell people, "Oh yeah, we had this violent fight." I'm embarrassed. But I also want people to know so they can tell me, "This is abuse." I don't want to have to figure it out myself.

Andrew doesn't hit me in the face. He doesn't slap me. He leaves no bruises to see. I never end up in the hospital. We yell at each other. He destroys things of mine that matter. How can it be abuse? Can it? I tell him, "I'm going to see a therapist."

"I'll be your therapist," he says.

The person who's causing the problem is the only one I can talk to about it. It's insane.

ATTENTION STARVED

I call a hotline. I get a number for a counselor, who runs a group for teen girls in abusive relationships. I show up at a meeting.

"You're attention starved," one of the girls says.

"And Andrew's abuse is attention," says another.

"You're asking your mom and dad to get involved in this drama," the counselor says.

I don't like the way the other girls gang up on me. They don't understand I come from a sophisticated background. Then the counselor starts saying, "Elizabeth, the abuse is about old stuff, too. Like your feelings about having famous parents or times when your dad would yell at you."

"Okay. I won't see Andrew anymore," I say. But that's to get them all off my case.

August 26, 1991, *Los Angeles Times.*

Surviving Abuse Like Hostages Do

The baffling problem of why abused women often remain in harmful relationships is undergoing a new appraisal by some mental health experts. They now say these women exhibit a behavior that can develop in classic hostage situations....

Among abused women, often the victim is grateful for any act of kindness the abuser shows her, denies the abuse, is hypervigilant to the abuser's needs, finds it difficult to leave the abuser and fears the abuser will come back to get her if she ends the relationship.

She sees this person as her only friend. This is also a person who has given her life. This is the only identity she has now. These feelings might be even more likely to develop in young women's dating relationships, experts say. One reason is that young women are more likely to perceive violence as evidence of love.

Things That Make Us Cry

Eric

Sometimes I **worried, "Am I crazy?"** I was **fifteen** and had actually **never** even **kissed a girl.** I was definitely **interested in changing that. Her name** was **Michelle.**

Six of us, including Michelle, were on a bus going to an environmental conference. My idea was to wait until the end to ask her out. That way, if she said no, I wouldn't have to feel stupid for the whole rest of the trip.

There I was, getting my confidence together, when this girl Liza calls out across a couple rows of seats, "Hey, Eric! You want to go to the Thanksgiving dance?"

Liza came with rumors and reputation: a brilliant crazy who went around with weird people. I looked at Michelle, trying to make an expression that said, I don't want to. But then I looked back at Liza and thought, "Maybe it'll be fun."

"Okay," I said.

CONTRACT

About our third time out, Liza and I got drunk in the graveyard and talked about things that made us cry.

She told me that about a month earlier, this guy she'd just met at the mall had raped her. "It's changed me," she said. "I don't want to ever have sex again."

I felt sorry for her and lost interest in Michelle. I said to Liza, "I'll prove to you that there are good people in the world."

We talked about our families. Her parents were always on her case. Even though my parents were divorced, they taught me morals: Help those who need help. Don't take more than my share of the pie. That sort of thing.

"It's hard to stick to your beliefs," Liza said.

She was right. We go to a traditional Alabama high school. Football is a big part of life. Homecoming and prom are important, too. But not for me. I volunteer for Greenpeace. I ran for class president on a platform of political issues.

"Do you think I'm crazy?" I asked her.

"No," she said. "You're just different from other guys. You're gentle and respectful." Then she confessed she thought I must not like her much. I didn't come on to her.

"Sure, I like you. I'm just shy." I didn't want her to know I was inexperienced.

Liza talked about her grades. They were outstanding. "But they're my only identification. Maybe now," she teased me, "I'll be known as Eric's girlfriend."

This whole time we'd been drinking. She told me she was the addictive type. She started to cry. "I wonder what it would be like if we both stopped drinking for good?" she said.

"Maybe we'd be able to deal with our feelings better," I said. "Why don't we sign a contract that we won't drink or use drugs?"

"Only if we seal it with a kiss," she said, and we did. Lisa's moods seemed to blow with the wind. Every hour with her was different.

LOVE

By Christmas, I'm walking her to class. Holding hands with her in the halls.

Sometimes we visit historic houses in town. We take photographs of each other with them in the background. We like to talk about politics, religion, and world peace. When we're alone, we have what Liza calls "kissing lessons." It's an excuse not to be embarrassed.

After that, I guess you can say we get more serious. I want to have sex, but I'm not going to even mention it. It's up to her.

We're spending more and more time in my room. When my mom's home, she's upstairs in her half of the house. Liza and I come and go, and she doesn't really notice. Mom's a modest person, too; she understands. She never comes in my room uninvited.

One afternoon during vacation, Liza says, "You know, Eric, if we make love, I'd consider it a recovery. I've regained confidence in males."

She started on the Pill.

LOVE

On a Thursday evening in January, Liza's mother finds the birth control pills. "You and Eric are over," she announces.

Liza calls me right away. "I don't know how I can live without you." I get emotional, too.

She says, "I'll call right back. I need to get some water. Don't do anything." I'm sitting there, not knowing what's really going on.

When she finally does call, she says her mom agreed we can get together, but with these rules: We can only see each other once a week. We are only allowed to be together if we are with other teenagers or a parent. We can never go into each other's bedroom ever again.

"I don't see any way out of these rules," Liza tells me.

The next time I call, her brother tells me, "She's in the hospital. She swallowed all these pills." I'm shocked.

I sneak into the hospital, up to intensive care, and stay with her a couple of hours. Three days later, I break the contract and start drinking again.

I feel Liza tried to end her life because of our love, and I didn't. During high school I swallow forty-eight of the same pills she has. I'm not going to tell anybody. I'll just go home, go to sleep, and never wake up.

But all of a sudden, in between classes, there's Liza! She is back in school talking about recovery. I don't know what to do. I shouldn't have, but I tell Liza what I've done.

Before she goes to her therapist appointment, she tells her mom what I did. By the time I get home, Liza and her mom show up. They take me to the emergency room. To make sure I go, they call my mom and the police, too.

At the hospital Liza asks the doctor, "Can I see Eric?"

When he tells her, "You've already caused him enough trouble," she starts shrieking, running up and down the hospital halls.

They take her to the top floor and commit her for depression. The next thing I know, they're taking me to another facility. They say, "We don't want you at the same hospital."

LOST TRUST

LOST FAITH,

I felt I was caged in. "You don't have any real problems," the therapist kept telling me. "You only went along with it. You copied Liza."

It was awful. In order to get out, I had to agree with what they said. Two weeks later, they let me go. Within a week Liza was out, too.

We'd been planning to go to the Valentine dance. "What about that?" I asked her.

"Oh, I'm going with Patrick."

"Break the date."

"No," she said. "Eric, if you want to know the truth, I lost faith in you when you tried to commit suicide. I wanted you there to support me. You were supposed to be the stable one."

"What?"

"Everybody's pressuring me not to see you. They blame you for the trouble we got in," she said.

"What!" I finally said.

"I don't trust you. You lied to me. You told me not to 'do anything,' then you tried to kill yourself."

I felt terrible. I didn't like her telling everybody what happened. I wanted to keep it a secret.

I escaped into sleep. My mom didn't press me much. She blamed Liza and didn't want us to be together anymore. She said, "There're better people in the world for you."

I was determined, though, to get Liza back. I called her, saying we had to talk.

She said, "No, and anyway, I don't think you're really capable of opening up to me."

That made me more upset. My mom told me that most men couldn't talk about their feelings. She wanted me to be able to.

She taught me through example. In a movie she'd point out when a male was angry, instead of talking about his feelings, he, like, jumped in his car and raced away. My mom would say, "Eric, it's better to face your emotions than run away."

FULL CIRCLE

Before all this, my mom and I talked a lot. After my breakup, I stopped talking to her.

Sometimes when I went out, I didn't come home all night. More and more I started drinking and doing drugs.

I missed Liza, even though I felt relieved without her. To get back my old life, I decided to have a party. I invited Liza, too. About forty people showed up, including her. She came with a girlfriend, but the girlfriend left.

Liza stayed and said, "Do you want me to hang around and help you clean up?" Things grew from there. Liza said, "Let's agree not to make any more promises, and seal it with a kiss." We did.

About two weeks later, we went to the movies. Liza was driving. In the car going home I criticized the main female character: "She was selfish, materialistic, and treated men badly. She liked to deal with men by holding power over them."

Liza took that all personally. I tried to explain to her that it was the movie, not her.

She didn't understand. She didn't care. She got all worked up. She stopped the car and said, "Get out." For me that was the end of the relationship. I walked home.

The next day I picked up the phone and called Michelle.

Michelle answered. "I'm going to an Earth Day planning session," I said. "Do you want to come along?"

"Okay," she said. "It'll give us a chance to get to know each other better."

Heartbreak on Valentine's Day

Yuelyne

I'M IN THE NINTH GRADE. MY FRIENDS ARE STARTING TO HAVE BOYFRIENDS, BUT I'M NOT LIKE THEM. I HAVE A DISABILITY. I WAS IN A CAST FOR YEARS. NOW I WALK WITHOUT LEG BRACES, BUT I WALK FUNNY.

ONE DAY MY FRIEND, DAWN, SAID:

YVELYNE, I THINK JAMIE LIKES ME.

I'M ASKING HIM TO THE VALENTINE'S DAY DANCE.

YOU AND JAROD MAKE A NICE COUPLE.

FASHION

HE'S SWEET TO ME AND WHEN I'D GET A HIT IN STREET BALL, HE'D ALWAYS RUN FOR ME.

SALE

HEY! WHAT'S GOING ON HERE?
DAWN, HE'S A CHICKEN! =WAAAA=
COME ON, YVELYNE, COME AWAY.
I'M NOT GOING TO THE DANCE! =SOB=
MY FRIENDS TALKED ME INTO GOING TO THE DANCE WITHOUT A DATE.
YVELYNE, WE'VE BEEN FRIENDS FOREVER. WE SHOULD GO TO THE DANCE TOGETHER.
DON'T WALK
I SAT ON THE SIDE-LINES WATCHING MY FRIENDS DANCE. I FELT AWFUL.

I Am Still Me

I am still me
without seeing you
I am still me
without being with you
I am still me
in a different form
I am still me
without having you
I am still me
looking in the mirror
I am still me
with all my set goals
I am still me
without you by my side
I am still me
without having you make it okay
I am still me
through my days
I am still me
without holding you
I am still me
alone as you see

Created for a class assignment
by Shira B. Ackerman
freshman, Edmund Burke School
Washington, D.C.

Part Three

THIS THING CALLED LOVE

TeAcheRs' aNd stuDeNtS' GuiDe To HeaRtBreaK aNd RoseS

Teachers contacted me to report how they used *Heartbreak and Roses* in their classrooms. I was intrigued by the ways they took the book's premise—a collection of compelling, real-life love stories—

and expanded it through group discussions and individual projects.

Diana Blitz, a Values Teacher at Edmund Burke School, Washington, D.C., was particularly helpful. She e-mailed me that "the school requires all the students in high school to take one trimester per year of Values. Each year has a different agenda, with the ninth graders focusing on sexuality." Blitz selected *Heartbreak* as the class "text."

Here is a combination of her suggestions, those of other teachers and some students' questions.

INITIAL DISCUSSION

Teenagers are often struggling with the notion of love, period, let alone troubled love. To get the class started you could discuss that emotionally when it comes to dating not everyone is at the same place at the same time. Relationships with friends are complicated enough without dealing with a boyfriend or girlfriend. Instead some students may opt to play basketball over daydreaming about a possible romance.

To keep the discussion going, you could also talk about these student-suggested questions:

- What qualities would you want in an ideal boyfriend or girlfriend?

- Does anyone help you make decisions about dating and love?

- How do you feel about your parents' wishes on the subject of dating?

- Would you go out with someone your friends objected to?

- What are your feelings about going out with someone from a different race, culture or religion?

After reading a story from Part Two:

- Role-play what you would say or do if you were the storyteller. For example when Bonnie's violent boyfriend says, "You break up with me, I'm going to kill myself," what would you do if you were Bonnie? Why do you think she has a hard time getting out of the relationship?

- Role-play what you would say or do if you were the storyteller's best friend and/or therapist. What would you do if he or she refused to open up to you?

- What issues do you have in common with the storytellers? Are there some problems that seem far removed from those you know?

➤ Create a project about dating or love in your life. It can be in any form, a short story, cartoon strip, single panel drawing, poem, crossword puzzle, letter to the authors of this book—let your imagination fly. See pages 8, 86 and 138 for real-life examples of student projects.

Janet Bode & Stan Mack
Franklin Watts
c/o Grolier Publishing
90 Sherman Turnpike
Danbury, CT 06816

WITH THANKS

Many thanks to our families and friends: Barbara Bode, Carolyn Bode, Phyllis Cadle, Lucy Cefalu, Kay Franey, Harriet and Ted Gottfried, Kathryn Kilgore, Kenny Mack, Peter Mack, Kerri Mahoney, Rosemarie and Marvin Mazor, Jane O'Reilly, Stephanie Ripple, Mike Sexton, Peggy Sexton and Deborah Udin.

Countless media specialists nationwide invited us into their schools to talk with students about our books. In turn, many of those individual teenagers volunteered to share their stories. If they hadn't been willing to open their lives, this book would not exist. With thanks and appreciation to all of them.

WHO'S WHO

Janet Bode's titles, including *Beating the Odds, Voices of Rape* and *Kids Still Having Kids,* have received numerous awards from such groups as the American Library Association, the International Reading Association and the National Council for Social Studies. *Different Worlds: Interracial and Cross-Cultural Dating* inspired a *CBS-TV Schoolbreak Special* which was a finalist for the NAACP Humanitas Award and a nominee for four daytime Emmies. *The Oprah Winfrey Show, Larry King Live* and *20/20* are just a few of the programs on which Bode has appeared to discuss today's issues.

Reporter/cartoonist **Stan Mack** has written and illustrated more than fifteen children's books, contributed regularly to such publications as *the New York Times, Natural History Magazine* and *Print,* and created weekly strips for the *Village Voice* and *Adweek* magazine. He and Bode are frequent collaborators. His latest book-length titles are: *Stan Mack's Real Life American Revolution* and *The Story of the Jews: A 4,000 Year Adventure.*